Variety of Life

Mollusks

Please visit our web site at: www.garethstevens.com
For a free color catalog describing Gareth Stevens Publishing's
list of high-quality books and multimedia programs, call
1-800-542-2595 (USA) or 1-800-387-3178 (Canada).
Gareth Stevens Publishing's fax: (414) 332-3567.

Library of Congress Cataloging-in-Publication Data

Richardson, Joy.
    Mollusks / Joy Richardson. — North American ed.
        p. cm. — (Variety of life)
    Includes bibliographical references and index.
    ISBN 0-8368-4507-2 (lib. bdg.)
    1. Mollusks—Juvenile literature. I. Title.
QL405.2.R53   2005
594—dc22   2004056757

This North American edition first published in 2005 by
Gareth Stevens Publishing
A WRC Media Company
330 West Olive Street, Suite 100
Milwaukee, Wisconsin 53212 USA

This U.S. edition copyright © 2005 by Gareth Stevens, Inc.
Original editions copyright © 1993 and 2003 by Franklin Watts.
First published in 1993 by Franklin Watts, 96 Leonard Street,
London EC2A 4XD, England.

Franklin Watts Editors: Sarah Ridley and Sally Luck
Franklin Watts Designer: Janet Watson
Picture Research: Sarah Moule

Gareth Stevens Editor: Dorothy L. Gibbs
Gareth Stevens Designer: Kami Koenig

Picture credits: Bruce Coleman, Ltd. – 7, 11, 15, 27; Frank Lane
Picture Agency – 19; Natural History Photographic Agency – cover,
25; Planet Earth Pictures – 3, 9, 13, 17, 21, 23.

Printed in the United States of America

1 2 3 4 5 6 7 8 9 09 08 07 06 05

Variety of Life

Joy Richardson

Mollusks

GARETH**STEVENS**
GS
PUBLISHING
A WRC Media Company

Contents

Assorted Mollusks 6

Boneless Bodies 8

Starting Life 10

Growing a Shell 12

A Big Foot 14

Sea Snails 16

On the Rocks 18

Buried in the Sand 20

Hinged Shells 22

Slugs 24

Octopus and Squid 26

Mollusk Facts 28

For More Facts 29

Glossary .30

Index 32

Words that appear in the glossary are printed in **boldface** type the first time they occur in the text.

Assorted Mollusks

Snails, slugs, oysters, limpets, squid, and octopuses are all different kinds of mollusks.

The first mollusks lived in seas and oceans many millions of years before dinosaurs roamed Earth.

Mollusks have soft bodies, and most of them have **shells**. Mollusk shells from long ago can still be found as **fossils embedded** in rocks.

These fossils are mollusks that lived on Earth millions of years ago. ➡

Boneless Bodies

Mollusks do not have any bones inside their bodies, so the bodies of mollusks are squashy and stretchy.

The main part of a mollusk's body is a **hump** that contains the animal's heart, stomach, and intestines. The hump is covered with a layer of **flesh** called a **mantle**.

A mollusk's head is as squashy and stretchy as its body. A slug can stretch out its **tentacles** or pull its head inside itself.

Slugs have eyes on the ends of their tentacles! ➡

Starting Life

Mollusks come from eggs.

Some kinds of mollusks lay eggs that float on the water like tiny bubbles. Other mollusks **fasten** their eggs onto stones or seaweed. Sea slugs lay their eggs in ribbons of jelly. Whelks lay their eggs in **clusters**.

Some mollusks carry their eggs with them. The eggs of some snails grow into tiny animals inside the parent's body.

A whelk's empty egg case looks like a sponge that has washed up on the beach.

Growing a Shell

Most mollusks have shells to protect their soft bodies.

A mollusk's shell comes from the mantle around the animal's hump. The mantle makes a chalky liquid that hardens, forming a shell.

As the mollusk grows, new layers or **spirals**, called **growth rings**, are added to the shell. A mollusk never **outgrows** its shell. The shell keeps growing with it.

This mollusk shell has some very colorful growth rings. ➡

A Big Foot

A snail is a mollusk that moves around on a big **foot**.

A snail's big foot makes **slime**, which helps the snail slide over the ground. **Muscles** that act like ropes can pull the foot all the way inside the snail's shell.

A snail lives inside a shell that **coils** into a spiral. The shell has a little point on it that shows where the shell started growing.

Snails can close off their shell openings with slime. A layer of slime over the shell opening helps a snail stick to **surfaces** and keeps the snail from drying out.

A snail leaves a trail of slime as it moves along. ➡

Sea Snails

Empty shells are washed up on beaches when the mollusks inside them have died. Some of these shells belonged to sea snails known as whelks.

A whelk moves around by stretching out its big foot and pulling itself along. To catch food, it attacks other creatures. A whelk's tongue is covered with tiny teeth, like the edge of a saw.

To breathe, a whelk pushes out a tube that brings clean water into its hump. **Gills** in the hump collect **oxygen** from the water. Like all animals, whelks need oxygen to stay alive.

This whelk is using its big foot to crawl across the muddy sand. ➡

On the Rocks

Some mollusks **cling** to rocks when the **tide** goes out.

A limpet uses its big foot to attach itself to a rock. The big foot **clamps** onto the rock like a **sucker**, and the limpet's cone-shaped shell closes over it.

When the tide comes in, the limpet lifts its shell and moves around on its foot, scraping seaweed off of rocks with its rough tongue.

Later, the limpet returns to **anchor** itself again — in exactly the same place!

Limpets keep their shells closed while the tide is out. ➡

Buried in the Sand

Some mollusks, such as razor clams, have double shells, with a **hinge** for opening and closing.

A razor clam lives in the sand. Its big foot pokes out of the end of its shell and **burrows** into the sand. Then the clam pulls the shell down after it.

A razor clam does not go looking for food. It sticks out two tubes above the sand. Water comes through one tube and goes into the animal's hump. Food is collected from the water before the water is pumped out through the other tube.

These shells that have washed up on a beach are the empty shells of razor clams.

Hinged Shells

Cockles, mussels, scallops, and oysters all have hinged shells.

A mussel ties itself down and stays in one place. Its big foot produces a thick liquid that hardens into strong, white threads.

Scallops can swim. Squirting water by flapping its shell open and closed pushes a scallop forward.

A scallop's many eyes can be clearly seen all around the opening of its shell. ➤

Slugs

Like a snail, a slug has a big foot, but slugs do not have shells.

Land slugs are dark and plain looking. They taste so nasty that no other animals even try to eat them.

Sea slugs are more **attractive**. They often have brightly colored **markings** or are covered with feathery **tufts**.

A sea slug's colorful markings warn enemies to keep away. Sea slugs can sting! ➡

Octopus and Squid

An octopus has powerful eyesight and a good brain — but it has no head!

All of an octopus's body parts are close together in a hump, covered by a mantle. An octopus has a mouth like a beak and eight tentacles lined with suckers for catching fish and crabs. When it is in danger, an octopus squirts out a cloud of ink to hide itself.

Squid are relatives of the octopus. Giant squid are the biggest mollusks in the world.

This octopus has its eight tentacles spread out to catch passing sea creatures. ➡

Mollusk Facts

There are all different kinds of mollusks in the world, but they are the same in many ways.

- All mollusks have soft bodies with no bones inside.

- Most mollusks have shells to protect their soft bodies. The shells often last longer than the mollusks inside them.

- Most mollusks live in water and have gills for breathing. Mollusks that live on land breathe air.

- Some mollusks hunt for food. Others collect food from the water that flows through their bodies.

For More Facts . . .

Books

Octopuses. Welcome to the World of Animals (series).
  Diane Swanson (Gareth Stevens)

Sea Slugs. Weird Wonders of the Deep (series).
  Valerie J. Weber (Gareth Stevens)

Sea Snails. Science under the Sea (series).
  Lynn M. Stone (Rourke)

Shellfish Aren't Fish. Rookie Read-About Science (series).
  Allan Fowler (Scholastic)

Web Sites

All About Snails — *www.kiddyhouse.com/snails/*

A Beginner's Introduction to Molluscs
  www.manandmollusc.net/beginners_intro/beginners_guide.html

Enchanted Learning Animal Printouts: Mollusks
  *enchantedlearning.com/subjects/invertebrates/
  mollusk/Printouts.shtml*

Glossary

anchor: (v) to hold in place

assorted: of different kinds

attractive: inviting; nice to look at

burrows: (v) digs a hole or a tunnel underground

clamps: (v) fastens by pressing together tightly

cling: to hold onto tightly

clusters: (n) groups in which objects are very close together

coils: (v) winds around in circles

embedded: set firmly into a surrounding surface

fasten: to attach

flesh: soft, meaty body tissue

foot: the large muscle on the underside of a mollusk's body, which spreads out and makes rippling movements to move the animal forward

fossils: outlines of plants and animals pressed into rock

gills: the body parts that make animals able to breathe underwater

growth rings: markings that show the number of growth periods an animal or a plant has lived through, with one ring for each growth period

hinge: (n) a movable joint, or place where two things are attached but can still turn or bend

hump: a rounded lump or raised area

mantle: the fleshy skin that wraps around the body organs in the humps of mollusks

markings: marks, especially particular shapes or patterns

muscles: the strong, stretchy tissues that make body parts able to move

outgrows: becomes too large for a particular space

oxygen: a colorless, odorless, tasteless gas that all animals need to breathe to stay alive

shells: hard outer coverings

slime: a thick, slippery, and sometimes sticky, liquid

spirals: series of connected circles, arranged one on top of another

sucker: an animal or object that clings to something by sucking out, or removing, the air in between

surfaces: top or outside layers

tentacles: long, thin, flexible body parts that help certain animals grasp, feel, move, and sometimes, see

tide: the daily rising or falling of the ocean's surface

tufts: small bunches of hairlike strands that are anchored together at the bottom but move around freely at the top

Index

beaches 10, 16, 20
bodies 6, 8, 10, 12, 26, 28
bones 8, 28
breathing 16, 28

cockles 22

eggs 10
eyes 8, 22, 26

food 16, 20, 28
foot 14, 16, 18, 20, 22, 24
fossils 6

gills 16, 28
growth rings 12

heads 8, 26
humps 8, 12, 16, 20, 26

limpets 6, 18

mantles 8, 12, 26
muscles 14
mussels 22

octopuses 6, 26
oysters 6, 22

razor clams 20
rocks (stones) 6, 10, 18

sand 16, 20
scallops 22
sea slugs 10, 24
sea snails 16
seaweed 10, 18
shells 6, 12, 14, 16, 18,
   20, 22, 24, 28
slime 14
slugs 6, 8, 24
snails 6, 10, 14, 24
squid 6, 26

teeth 16
tentacles 8, 26
tides 18
tongues 16, 18

water 10, 16, 20, 22, 28
whelks 10, 16